Tools Scientists Use

Sarah Russell

Scientists observe and measure things.
They try to understand how things work.

Scientists use many tools to help them do their job.

A **microscope** is a tool some scientists use.
A microscope makes very small things
look bigger.
A scientist uses a microscope to observe
blood cells.

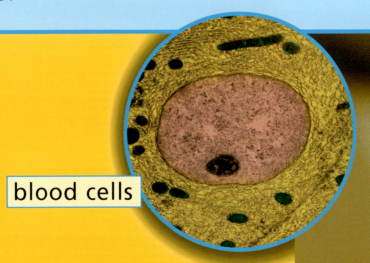

blood cells

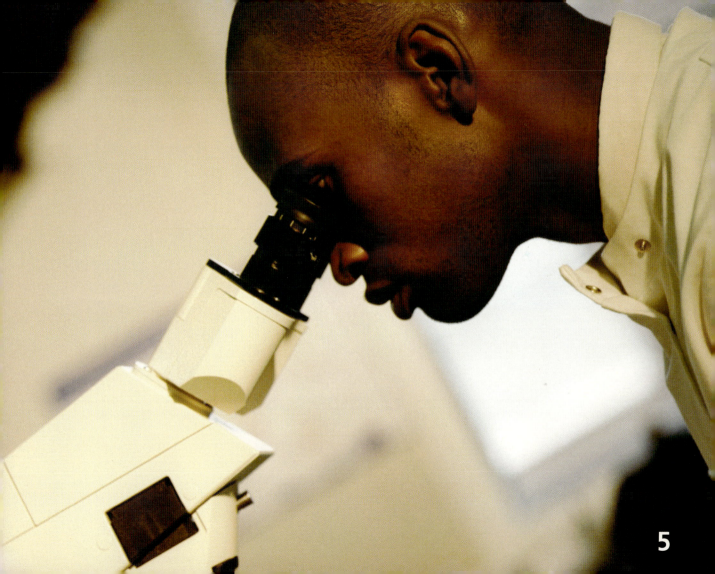

A **telescope** is a tool some scientists use.
A telescope makes things that are far away look closer.
A scientist uses a telescope to observe stars in space.

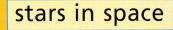

stars in space

6

A **hand lens** is a tool some scientists use. A hand lens makes it easier to see details on small things.
A scientist uses a hand lens to observe plants.

9

A **ruler** is a tool some scientists use. A ruler measures the size of things. A scientist uses a ruler to measure the size of different animals.

A **rain gauge** is a tool some scientists use.
A rain gauge measures rainfall.
A scientist uses a rain gauge to measure how much rain has fallen in an area.

13

A **computer** is a tool some scientists use.
A computer stores information.
A scientist uses a computer to find answers to problems.

Index